THIS BOOK BELONGS TO

_____

MATTEO GUARNACCIA
DAVID BOWIE PLAY BOOK

COLOUR, CUT, PLAY!

EDITED BY
GIULIA PIVETTA

THIS PLAY BOOK WAS CREATED BY THE AUTHOR
WHILE LISTENING EXCLUSIVELY TO DAVID BOWIE'S
MUSIC ON SHUFFLE AND PLAYED AT FULL VOLUME!

© ACC Art Books Ltd, 2016
World copyright reserved
ISBN: 978-1-85149-842-0

Originally published in Italian by 24 ORE Cultura srl, Milan

Art direction and layout by Alice Beniero

English language translation by Sylvia Notini

British Library Cataloguing-in-Publication Data
A catalogue record for this book is available from the British Library

Printed and bound in China for ACC Editions,
an imprint of ACC Art Books Ltd., Woodbridge, Suffolk, UK

"ABSOLUTES ARE OBSOLETE"

EVER-ENCHANTING

EVER-CHANGING

DAVID BOWIE

SO MANY CH·CH·CH·CH·CHANGES

It is neither an easy nor a predictable task to tell the story of one of the most original contemporary artists ever, especially when you're dealing with a guy from London of alien descent, or, contrariwise, someone who admitted to reinventing his image so many times that even he "was in denial that [he] was originally an overweight Korean woman".

I was experiencing the pleasant feeling of forcefully being pulled back into the orbit of his relentless intelligence, of his ability to be "naturally" artificial in both his music and his style. I was already halfway through my project, listening to nothing but Bowie, immersed in his world of sounds – I was working on a drawing of his face –, when I heard the news about his departure from Planet Earth. It was an event of pure synchronicity, the feeling that some sort of magical connection had been created. The first thing that came to my mind was that it had to be some outrageous prank: the Starman, the Pierrot of All Sexes, had fooled me again. Like in 1972, when the epiphanic vision of Ziggy forced me to abandon my folk-psychedelic look and tune into the Space Oddity instead – mascara to highlight my eyes, a pair of silver spray-painted boxing boots on my feet. I will never be able to thank him enough for having cross-fertilized the free-range world of pop music with intellectual sophistication, and the self-referential snobbish world of art with the folly of rock.

M.G.

TABLE OF CONTENTS

A GAME OF DICE WITH STYLE

GIULIA PIVETTA

Throughout his career, David Bowie always stayed away from scripts that were imposed by others, choosing instead, for better or for worse, to be his own scriptwriter. His approach to rock 'n' roll was original, typically theatrical, and he would identify with and play the part of different characters each time, emphasizing before anyone else did the affinities between this revolutionary musical genre and Commedia dell'Arte. From the Sixties to the day he passed away, Bowie created a series of fictitious characters, imagining them, conceiving them, and transferring them to the stage, giving each one of them a specific personality.

Before reaching what would unanimously be acknowledged as the peak of his art, Ziggy Stardust, Bowie had never succeeded in going beyond the role of the average pop singer, one of many in the vast population of musicians that Great Britain was offering to the world, from Beatlemania to the many fads that followed. Though he'd tried in every way to do so, Bowie had never managed to make a name for himself. And yet he continued to nurture great ambitions in his profession. His goal was to become a star, a status for which there is no halfway house. To achieve this he soon realized that his stage costume could play a crucial role. Besides the traditional work of the actor and – needless to say – the author (endowed with a voice graced with the delicate and deep tones of a crooner), his vision also included costume design. At first, the costumes Bowie chose appealed to him for their practical function, the fact that he could use them to characterize the characters on stage. Later, this technical necessity grew somewhat more complex. Through his costumes, Bowie played a game of dice with fate: ever-changing disguises that became increasingly perfect, studied specifically for each new version of himself. It was thanks to this

endless change of register that Bowie developed the unique approach to aesthetics that characterized his work all the way to the last album he cut, Blackstar. In Bowie's work nothing was left down to chance: his plan was meticulous and extreme, and his attention to detail was raised to the nth degree in his spectacular and dramatic departure from the world accompanied by the enigmatic video he left as his legacy for his many admirers. Bowie always knew exactly what he was talking about, every change in style was the result of study, trial, and elaboration.

It's almost impossible to distinguish the boundary between Bowie's quest for style and his existential quest: he started out with jazz, played halls, pubs, and clubs, embraced rockabilly, and moved on to his own easy-going interpretation of dandyism (a word that's overused today, but that suits him to a T). Bowie was a member of the Peacock Revolution of the Sixties, the second wave of the British dandies, young "peacocks" who, like Bowie, trod the paths already beaten by Oscar Wilde and friends, wearing red or golden coats with silver buttons and big patch pockets. One of Bowie's specialties was casting aside his masks, even when they were successful, before they became clichés – from the disposable fashion sold in boutiques like Mr. Fish on Carnaby Street, to the Japanese performance-fashion of Kansai Yamamoto. From one style to another, the theatre was the place where everything converged, whether it was street theatre, mime, the stage used by the Bauhaus for its performance art, or the spectacular excesses of Japanese Kabuki. It is indeed a characteristic of Kabuki dance-drama to emphasize gestures, make-up, and costumes until they become grotesque, as well as indulging in sexual identity, allowing men to play female roles. In his long and fruitful career, David Bowie honed his style in the decade that ran from 1965 to 1975. That period deserves further study, and we can expect some surprises.

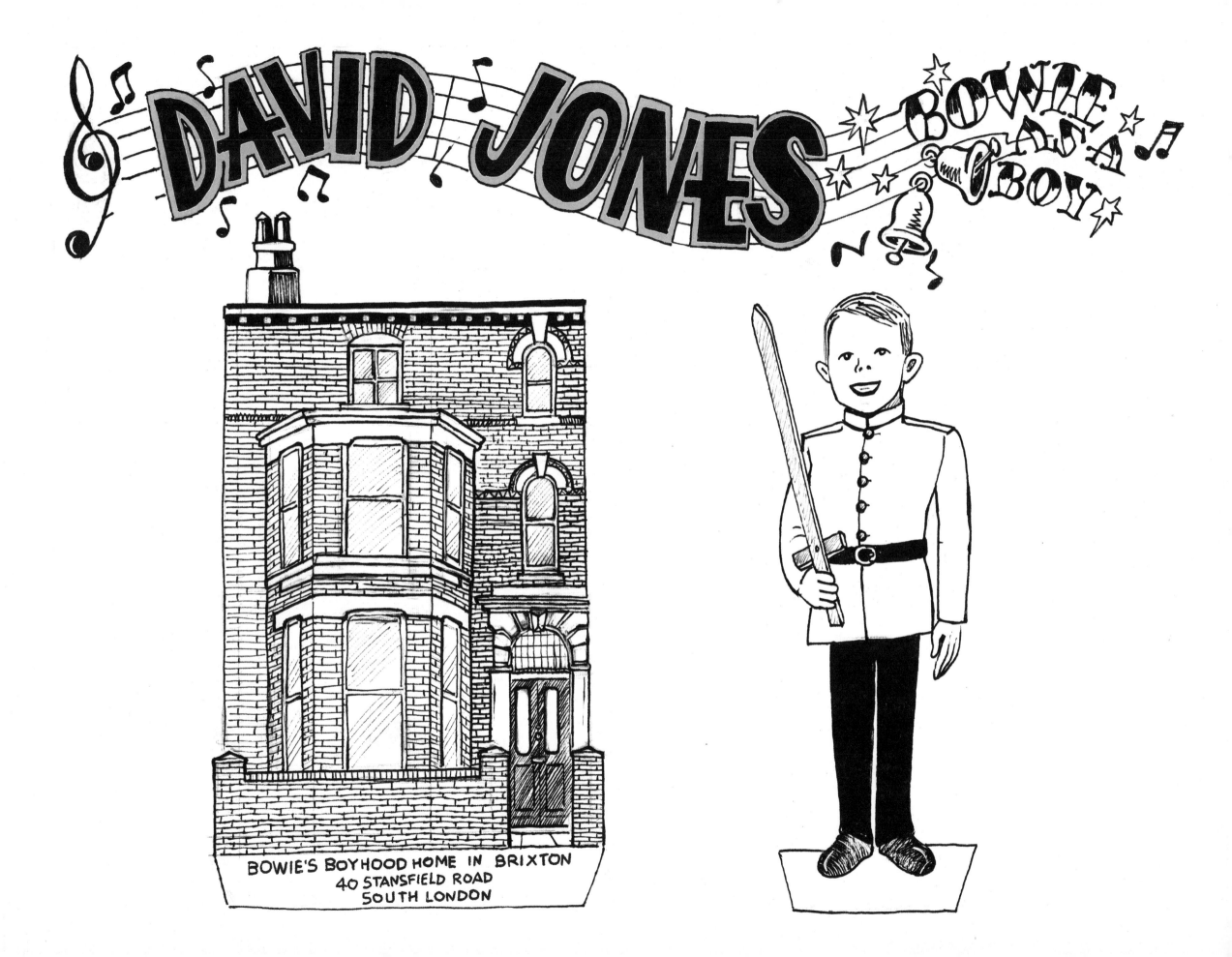

POINTY HEAD

ELF EARS

DAVID'S PLAYGROUND: BOMBED-OUT CHASMS AND HOUSES DESTROYED BY THE AIR RAIDS

Fabulous 208 David

THE WEST'S GREATEST FIGHTER

ALL NEW

JIM BOWIE

APPROVED BY THE COMICS CODE AUTHORITY

JIM BOWIE

10¢

inspired by a 19th-century legend of the Far West, Jim Bowie, inventor of an extra-large knife

MONKEES

It was future member of the Monkees Davy Jones's rise to fame as an actor that encouraged our hero to change his name to..

David Bowie

hippie style

CUT

Dylan style

GLUE HERE!

From **1964** (the year he refused to appear on the BBC show "Gadzooks! It's All Happening" if the producers forced him to cut his hair), to **1972** B.Z. (Before Ziggy) young David was always very proud of his mane.

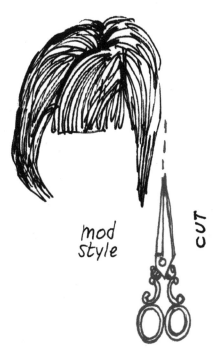

mod style

CUT

LA GIOCONDA CAFÉ AT 9 DENMARK St., SOHO LONDON - A FAMOUS HANG-OUT FOR MUSIC LEGENDS. THIS IS WHERE DAVID BOWIE MET THE MEMBERS OF HIS GROUP THE LOWER THIRD, ALONG WITH MARC BOLAN, ROD STEWART, RAY DAVIES, ETC.

...ALWAYS AN AVID READER...

DRESS CODE: MOD

"A London boy, oh a London boy. Your flashy clothes are your pride and joy!"

AND THE

DAVIE JONES

DEATH

LES

DAVIS

LOWER THIRD

handbill for David's band

JOHN STEPHEN BOOTS →

FAB fashion

CORDUROY
BELL-BOTTOMS

THIS WAY TO HIPPIELAND

JERSEY SHIRT

right

left

david girls 1

hermione farthingale

The girl with the mousy hair...

Letter to Hermione

BOWIE THE MIME:
CUT OUT THE BODY,
ARMS AND LEGS,
THEN CUT OUT THE HOLES
AND USE PAPER
FASTENERS TO CONNECT
THE PARTS.

david girls

Bowie's hippie years

The guru (and part-time lover) who taught David about stagecraft and the art of mime

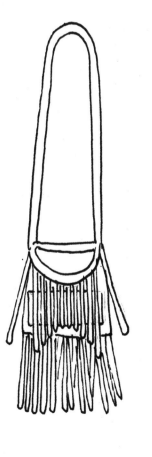

The Underground Mime Troupe

LINDSAY KEMP

1967
1969

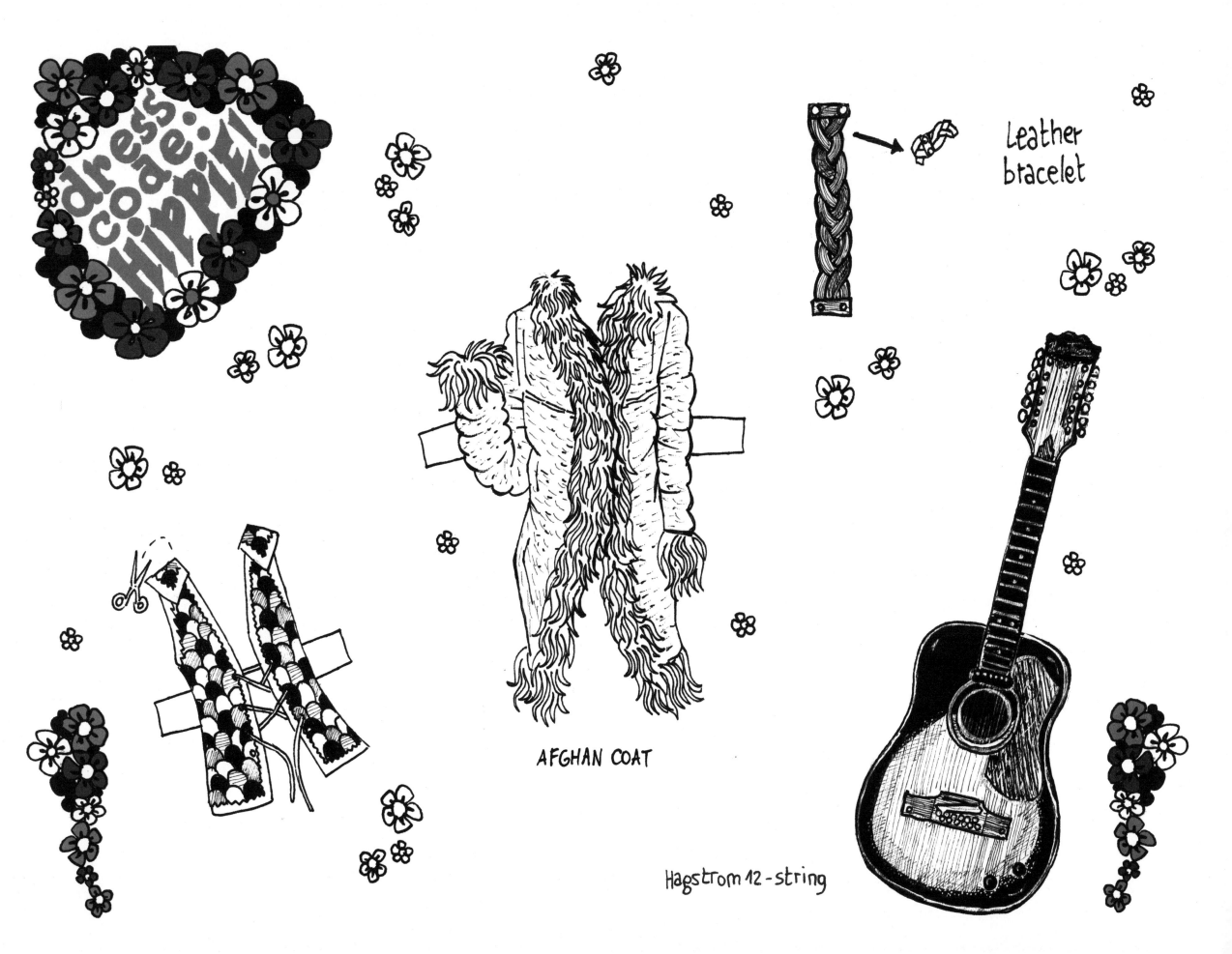

dress code: HIPPIE!

Leather bracelet

AFGHAN COAT

Hagstrom 12-string

PUFF SLEEVES!

Growth Summer Festival
and Free Concert.

— Beckenham Arts Lab —
Saturday 16th August

NOON to 8.00 pm

SOUNDS

John Peel, Bridget St. John, Sun.
Gas Works, Keith Christmas, Strawbs.
Miscarriage, Amory Kane, Hamirah.
Oswald K., Dave Jones, Junior Eyes.
Nita, David Bowie, Giles & Abdul.
Comus, Gun Hill... and others.....

STALLS

Barbecue, Exotic Tea Stall
and original Artwork, Candy
Magazine and Paper Shop,
Jewellery and Ceramics,
Street Theatre. Fuzz-nut
Mystics....and more...

Non-stop music and discs.
BECKENHAM RECREATION GROUND
Croydon Road, Beckenham
oooOooo

Those were the days, my friend... Hey! David Bowie's name on the handbill is the same size as the word "barbecue"!

1969

THE BAND-STAND WHERE THE ARTISTS PERFORMED

MEMORY·OF·A·FREE·FESTIVAL

Arts Lab button

Underground magazine buttons

On August 16, while 500,00 hippies were converging on Woodstock (NY), Bowie was arranging a free concert to encourage donations to the Beckenham Arts Lab, a counterculture enclave in south-east London

DAVID 2 GIRLS

ANGELA 'angie' BARNETT

The Prettiest Star

his First wife! It was she who led David Bowie down a dead-end street of sartorial provocation, sharing a marriage with him that was definitely open!

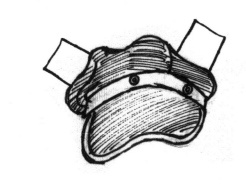

LIZARD RING

fancy black Basque beret

ZODIAC NECKLACE AND BROOCHES

short fur jacket

RAIDING HIS WIFE'S WARDROBE

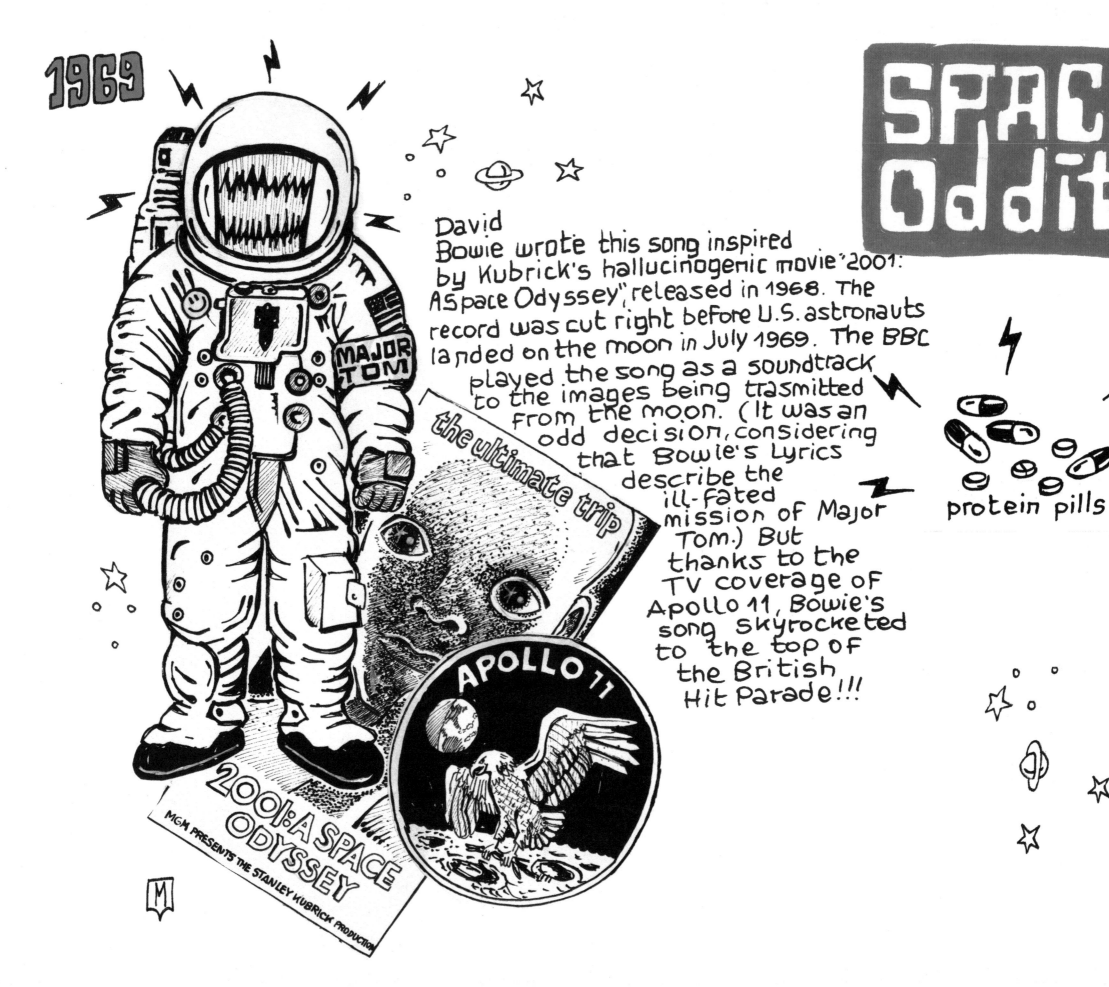

1969

SPACE Oddity

David Bowie wrote this song inspired by Kubrick's hallucinogenic movie "2001: A Space Odyssey", released in 1968. The record was cut right before U.S. astronauts landed on the moon in July 1969. The BBC played the song as a soundtrack to the images being transmitted from the moon. (It was an odd decision, considering that Bowie's Lyrics describe the ill-fated mission of Major Tom.) But thanks to the TV coverage of Apollo 11, Bowie's song skyrocketed to the top of the British Hit Parade!!!

protein pills

the ultimate trip

APOLLO 11

2001: A SPACE ODYSSEY

MGM PRESENTS THE STANLEY KUBRICK PRODUCTION

MAJOR TOM

SPACE Oddity

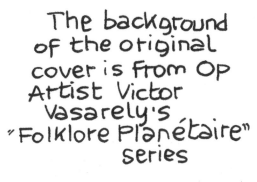

The background of the original cover is from Op Artist Victor Vasarely's "Folklore Planétaire" series

THERE IS LIFE ON MARS!!!

MAJOR TOM FAN CLUB

DAVID BOWIE

SPACE ODDITY

"The Man Who Fell To Earth" 1976 – Nicolas Roeg

DRESS CODE: A STEP AHEAD!?!

DAVID BOWIE CAME A LONG WAY FROM WHEN HE WAS A SIXTEEN-YEAR-OLD MUSICIAN

WITH A FABULOUS ROCKABILLY POMP WHO PLAYED THE SAXOPHONE IN A BAND CALLED The Kon-rads

IN **1971** STANLEY KUBRICK'S FILM ADAPTATION OF ANTHONY BURGESS'S NOVEL "A CLOCKWORK ORANGE" INTRODUCED THE STYLE OF THE MEAN **DROOGS** THAT WOULD INSPIRE **ZIGGY**'S LOOK!

1973

ANGEL OF DEATH

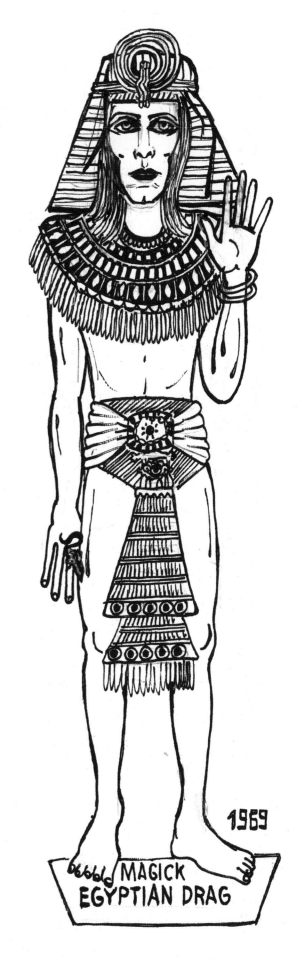

1969

MAGICK EGYPTIAN DRAG

Hagstrom/
Kent PB-24-G
electric guitar

SNAKESKIN BODYSUIT

OSTRICH
FEATHER BOA

ASYMMETRIC
KNITTED
BODYSUIT

LACE-UP
BOXING BOOTS

The Golden Years of a Fashion Junkie

COSTUME FOR THE ALADDIN SANE TOUR 1972-73

Bau haus
OSKAR SCHLEMMER das triadische ballet 1922

COLOURFUL, FUN POP OUTFITS DESIGNED BY KANSAI YAMAMOTO

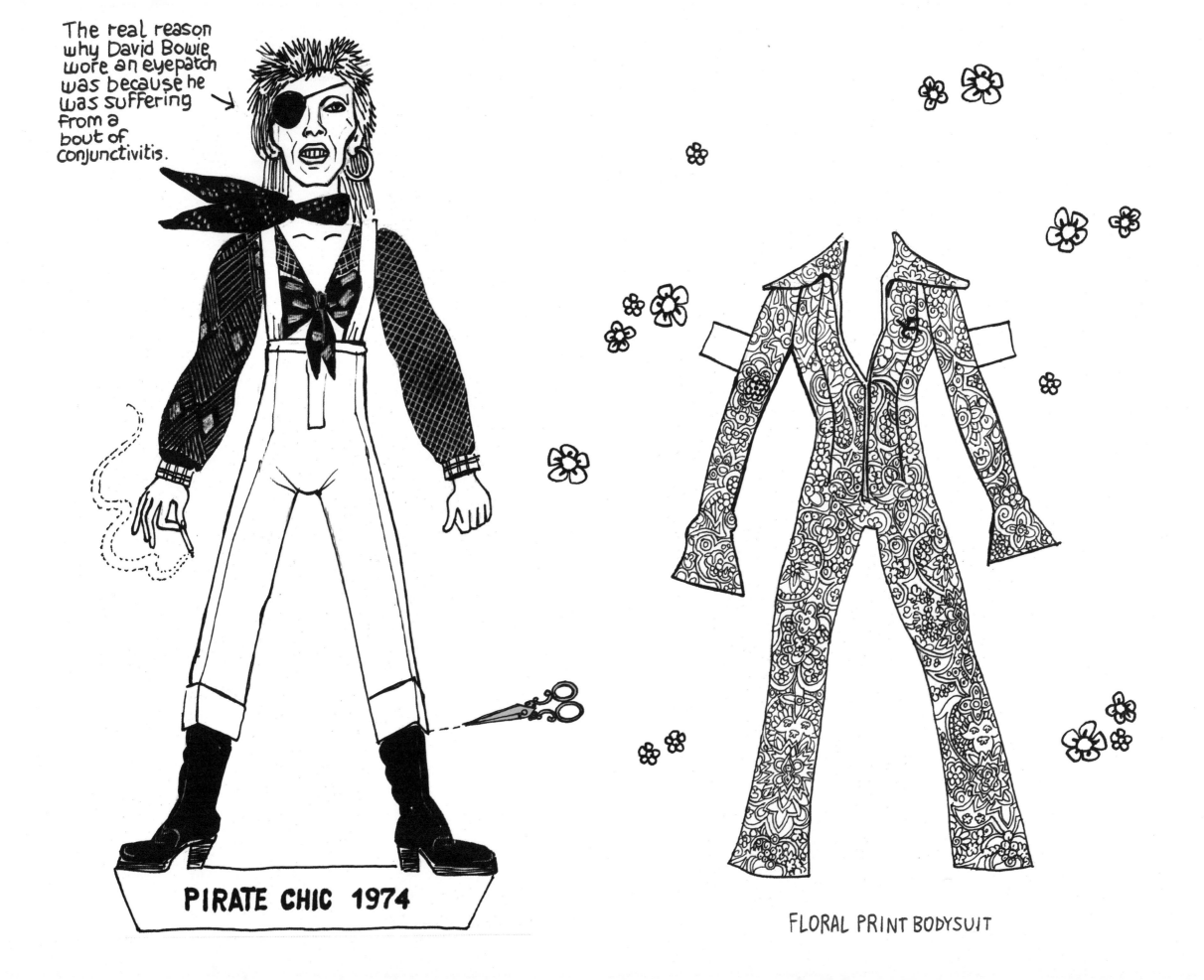

The real reason why David Bowie wore an eyepatch was because he was suffering from a bout of conjunctivitis.

PIRATE CHIC 1974

FLORAL PRINT BODYSUIT

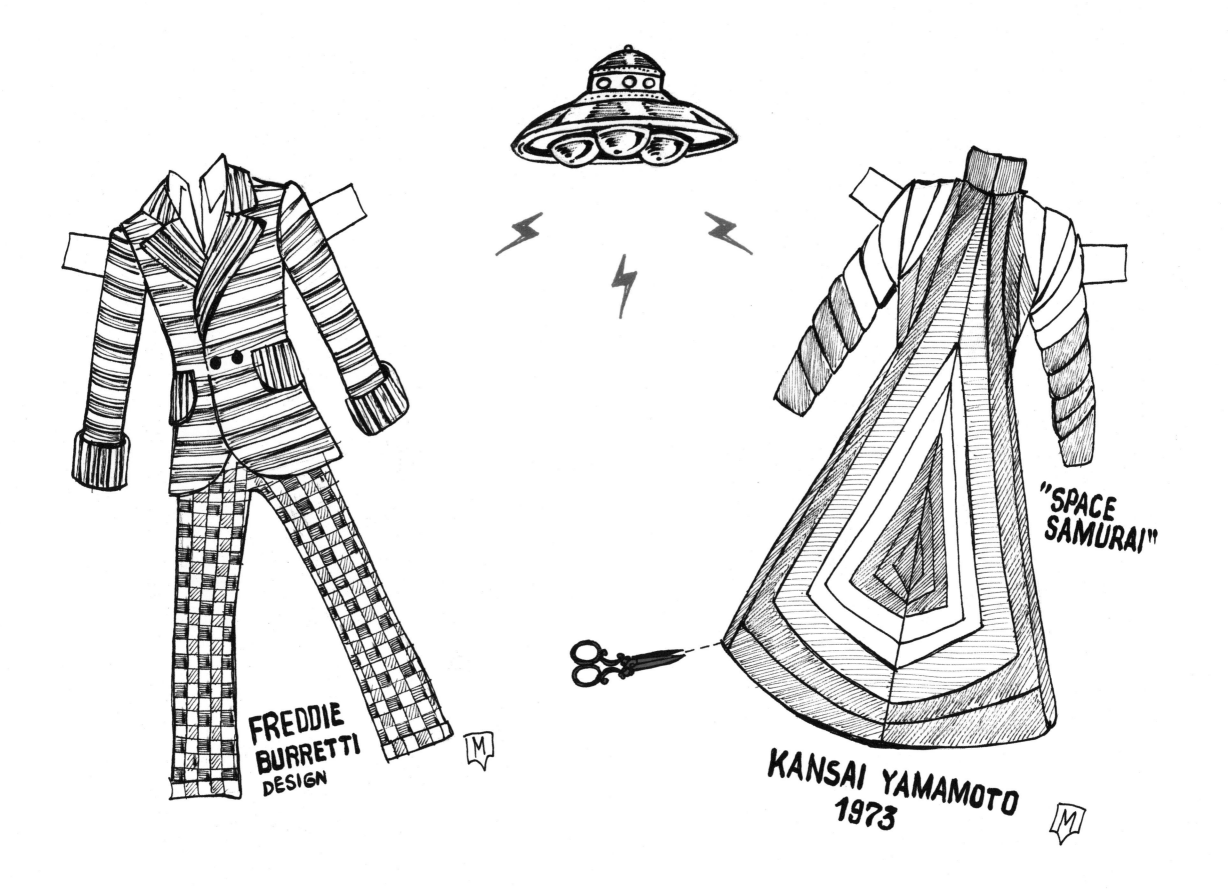

FREDDIE
BURRETTI
DESIGN

"SPACE
SAMURAI"

KANSAI YAMAMOTO
1973

FREDDIE
BURRETTI
1973

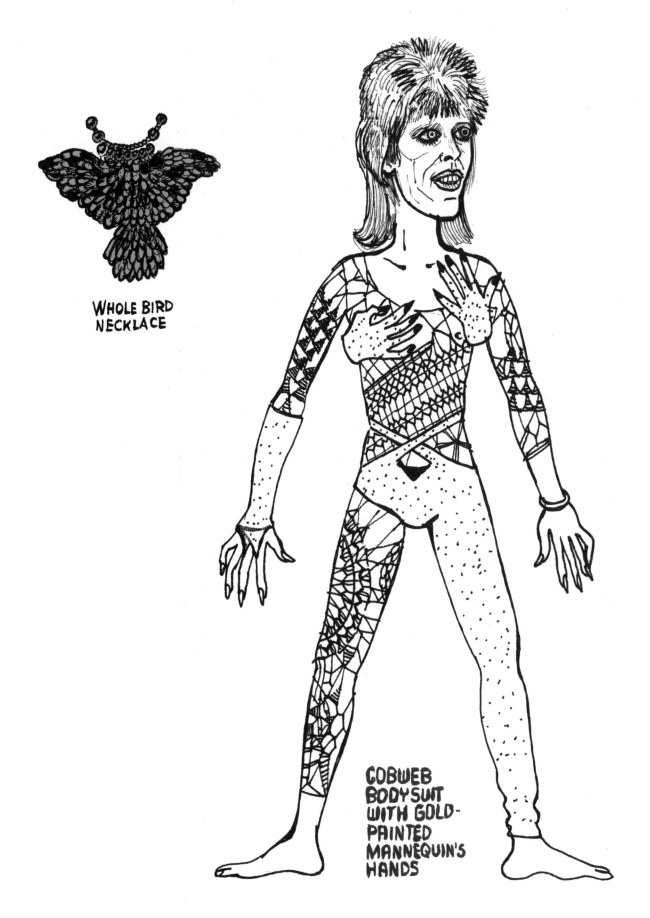

WHOLE BIRD
NECKLACE

COBWEB
BODYSUIT
WITH GOLD-
PAINTED
MANNEQUIN'S
HANDS

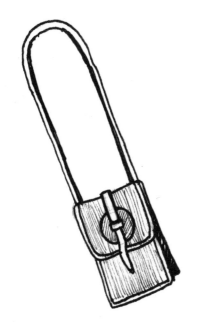

LEATHER HANDBAG

RED SEQUINED JOCKSTRAP

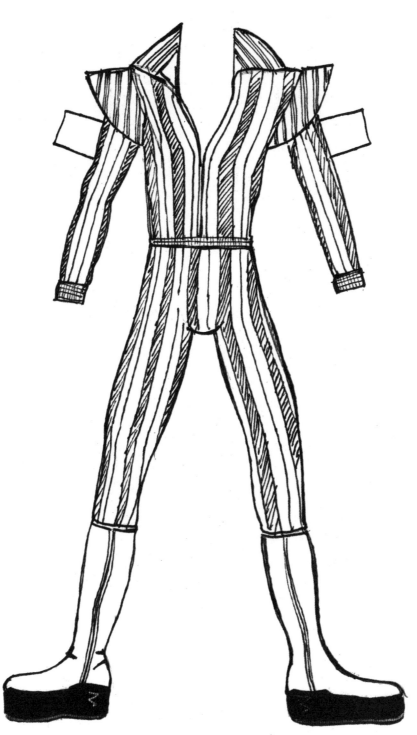

'SPACE ODDITY'

SPACE SUIT

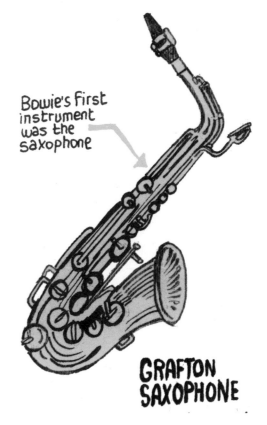

Bowie's first instrument was the saxophone

GRAFTON SAXOPHONE

When he was 13, David's father bought him a sax

YAMAMOTO

'SHORT
WHITE
SATIN
KIMONO
WITH
QUILTED
MOCK
TURTLE-
NECK AND
WHITE
KNEE-HIGH
SATIN
BOOTS'

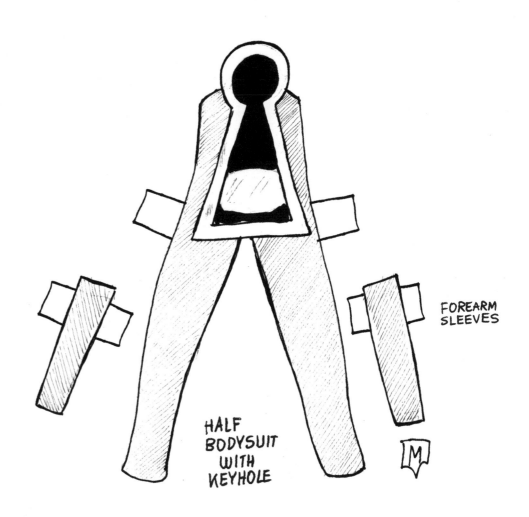

FOREARM
SLEEVES

HALF
BODYSUIT
WITH
KEYHOLE

STYLOPHONE
retro pocket
synthesizer

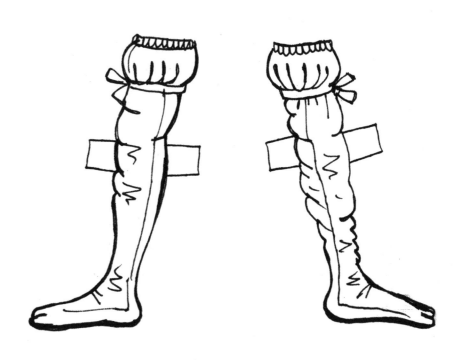

SHOE SHOW

1970

1973
PINUPS

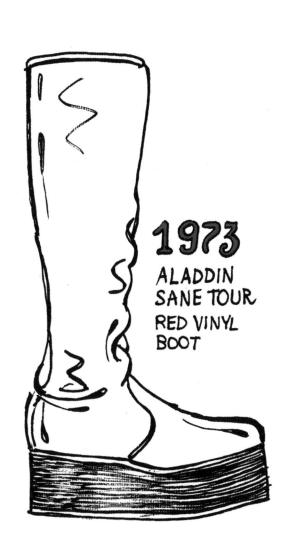

1973
ALADDIN
SANE TOUR
RED VINYL
BOOT

1973
YAMAMOTO
CREATION

1973
FREDDIE
BURRETTI
CREATION

1972
ZIGGY

1972

1973
YAMAMOTO
CREATION

1972
ZIGGY

1973

PVC "ANGEL OF DEATH"
THIGH-HIGH STILETTO
BOOT

1980 ASHES
TO
ASHES

1975
SOUL TRAIN

SHOESNOW

BOWIE GIRLS GROUPIES

The Wild and Amazing Nymphets of L.A.

A TRAILBLAZER IN THE SEXUALLY BOLD 70'S

Rodney Bingenheimer's

ENGLISH DISCO

"AN ISLAND OF ENGLISH 'NOWNESS' IN LOS ANGELES" (SAID DAVID BOWIE) – THE HAUNT OF GLAM ROCK GROUPIES
8171 SUNSET – WEST HOLLYWOOD

Here Comes Trouble! Los Angeles Groupies in full regalia 1972/1975

CUT OUT THE
DISCS, MAKE A
HOLE IN THE
MIDDLE OF EACH ONE,
PLACE ONE DISC ON TOP
OF THE OTHER, THEN
INSERT A PAPER FASTENER
THROUGH BOTH
HOLES!

ACHTUNG!!!

⚡1976⚡

Thin

White Duke

...and what about his Unhealthy passion for fascism (he weighs a mere 41 Kilos...that's 90 lbs.)

dress code: nazi-chic

In 1976 Bowie was detained on the Russian-Polish border where border guards seized his collection of Nazi books and memorabilia!!

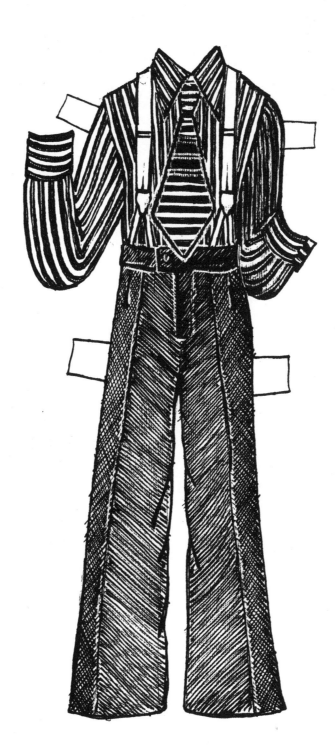

BERLIN (D) Hauptstrasse 155
Home to Bowie and Iggy Pop
1976 - 1978

155

a selection of

DAVID BOWIE

the people who most inspired him

IT'S NOT WHERE YOU TAKE THINGS FROM — IT'S WHERE YOU TAKE THEM TO...
— Jean-Luc Godard

Campbell's CONDENSED TOMATO SOUP

MY FAVOURITE DAVID BOWIE SONGS

1 _____

2 _____

3 _____

4 _____

5 _____

6 _____

7 _____

8 _____

9 _____

10 _____

DRAW YOUR OWN DAVID BOWIE